Earth

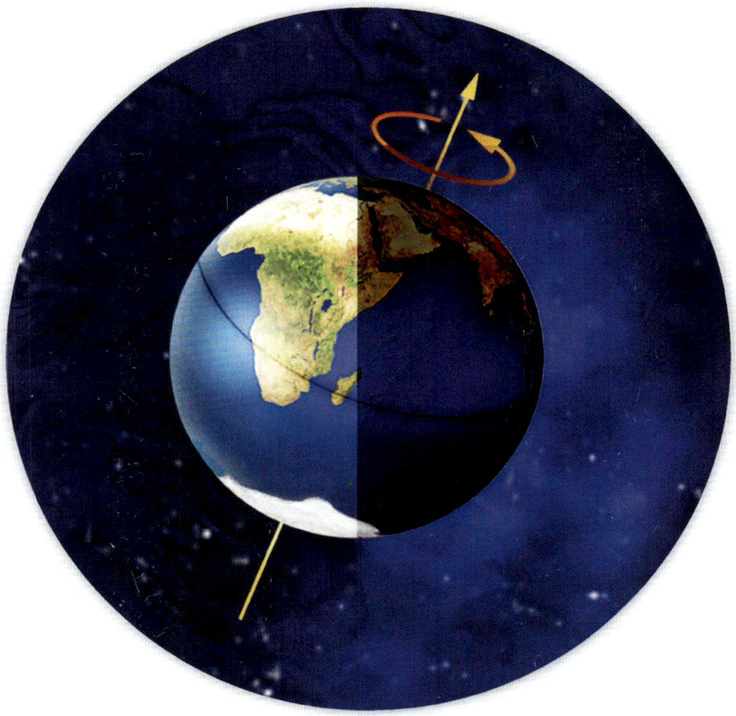

Written by Phillip Simpson

macmillan education

Contents

Earth's Movement

Did you know that the Earth is always moving? The Earth is circling around the Sun. It is also slowly spinning around. This is why it looks as though the Sun appears in the morning and disappears in the evening. But the Sun does not move.

The movement of the Earth is the reason why we have night and day, different seasons and a birthday every year. So how does it work?

We see the sun rise and set because of the movement of Earth.

Earth's Spin

We have night and day because the Earth is always turning on its **axis**. This is an imaginary line that the Earth turns around. Earth's axis runs from the North Pole to the South Pole.

It takes the Earth twenty-four hours to make one complete turn or **rotation**. We call this one day. When the Earth is facing towards the Sun, it is day. When the Earth is facing away from the Sun, it is night.

It is daytime in the half of Earth that faces the Sun.

In the past, many cultures created stories and legends about the Sun. A Dreaming story from Indigenous Australia tells how the Sun was made by a spirit. The spirit told a kookaburra to laugh loudly each morning so that those who slept could wake to enjoy the light. Other cultures imagined the Sun as a powerful god or goddess.

Rays of light shaped like lotus flowers shone from the sun disc on the head of Ra, the ancient Egyptian sun god.

Time Zones and Dates

When people travel to another country or state, sometimes they have to change the time on their phones and watches when they arrive. This is because the time is different in different places on Earth. We can tell the time in a different area by looking at which time zone it is in.

Earth is split into time zones using imaginary lines. The zones are spaced out around Earth. All places in a time zone keep the same time. Each time zone is one hour apart. For example, Beirut, Lebanon, is eight time zones away from Melbourne, Australia. When it is 9.00 am in Beirut, it is 6.00 pm in Melbourne.

Time Zones and the International Date Line

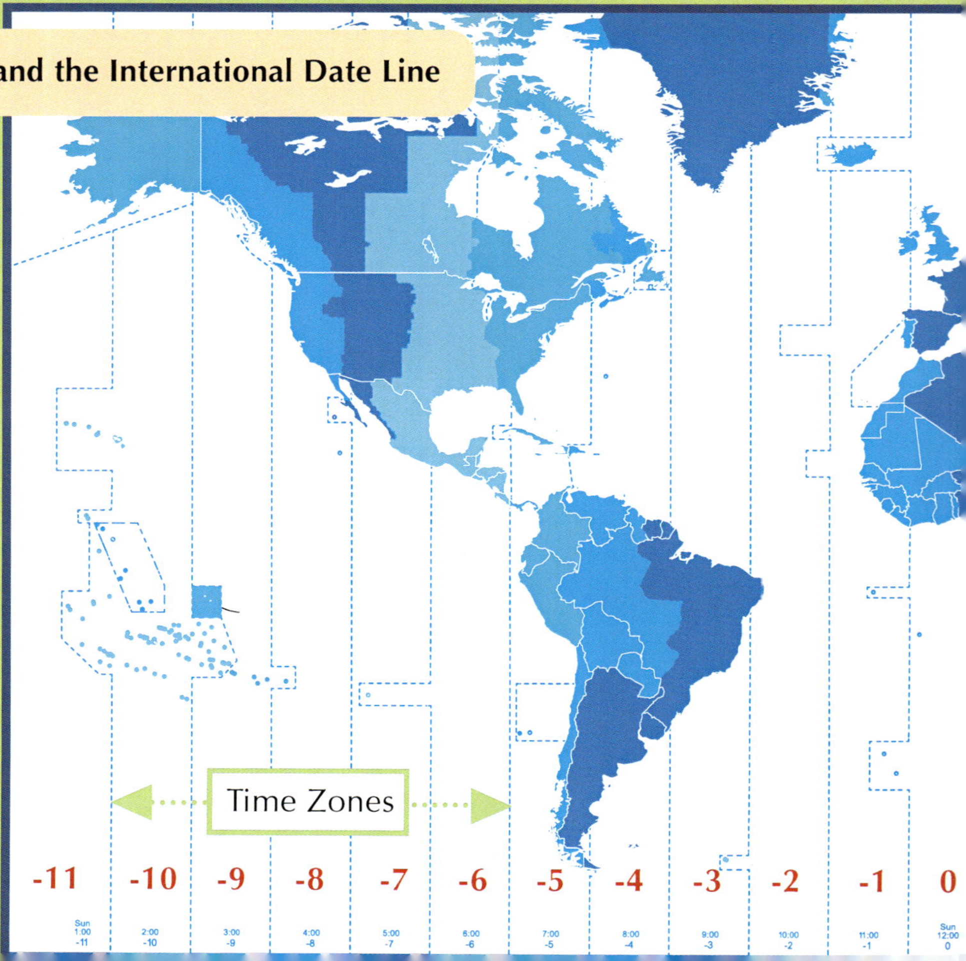

The International Date Line is another imaginary line. It marks where the date changes from one day to the next. It runs through the middle of the Pacific Ocean. It is a different date on either side of this line. For example, it might be night in both areas, but east of the line it is Tuesday night and west of the line it is Wednesday night! By crossing back and forth across the International Date Line, people can pretend they are time travellers!

Each New Year, New Zealand celebrates before other places because it is closer to the International Date Line.

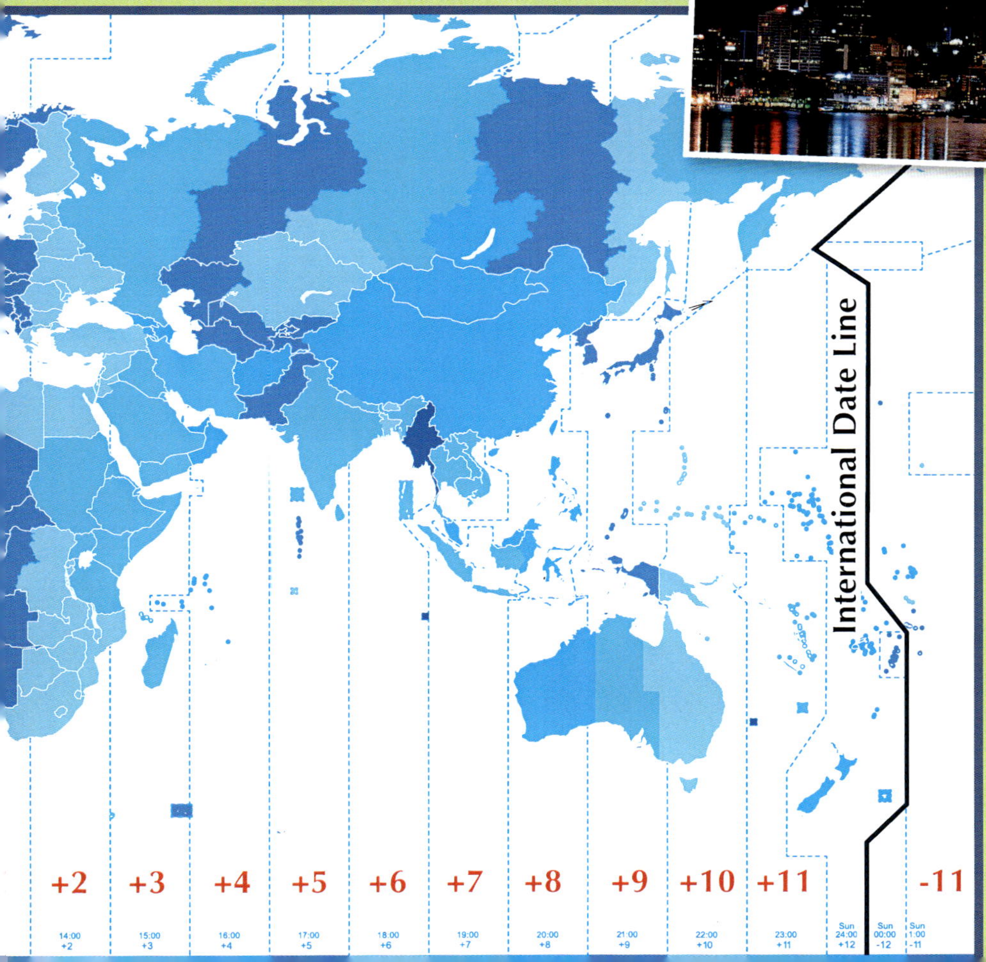

Earth's Orbit

The Earth **orbits,** or circles around, the Sun. It takes exactly 365 days, 5 hours, 48 minutes and 46 seconds for the Earth to complete one full orbit of the Sun. The exact time it takes for the Earth to orbit the Sun once is called a **solar** year. A solar year is just a few hours longer than a **calendar** year.

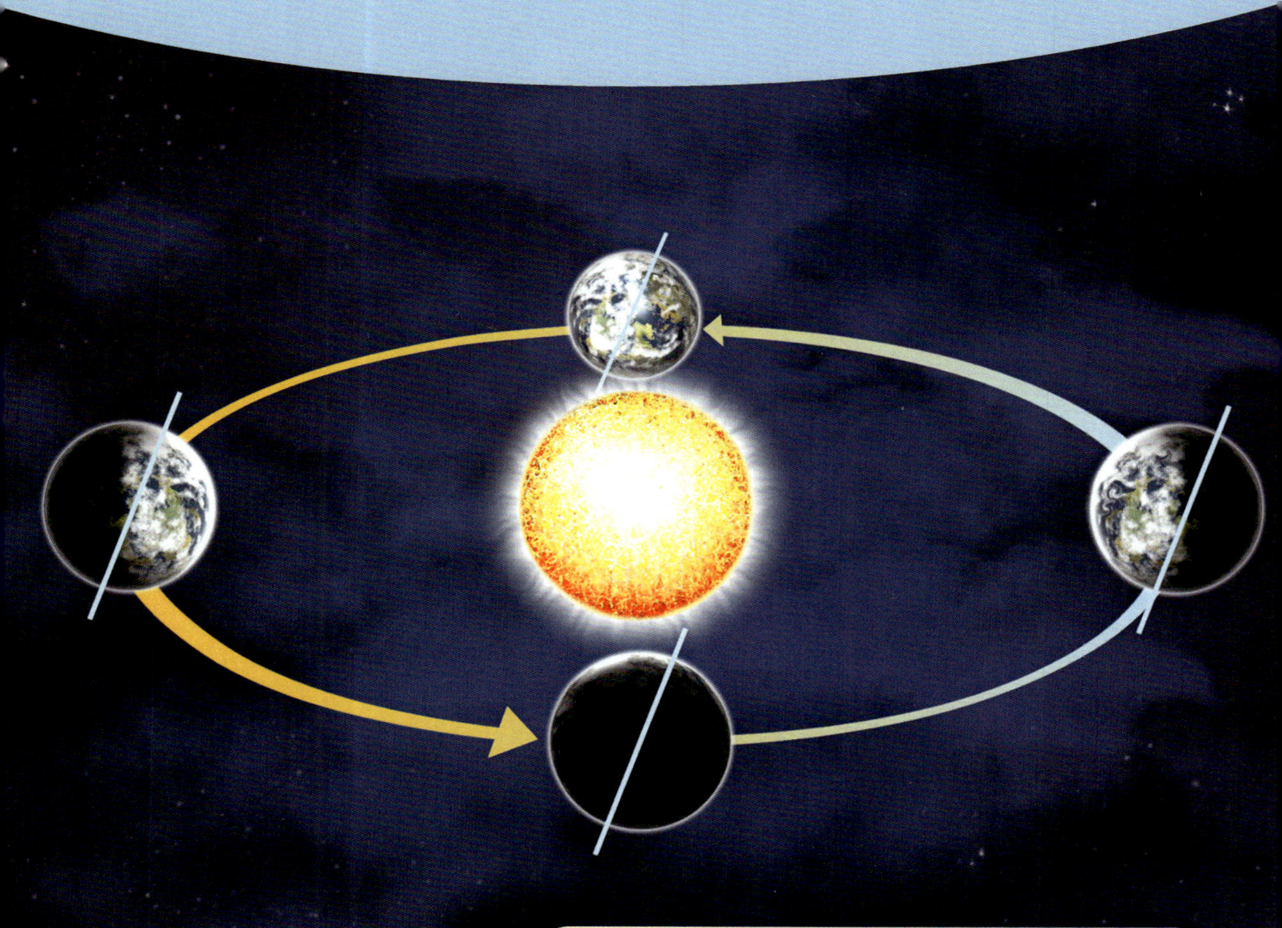

The Earth travels 149 600 000 kilometres in its year-long orbit around the Sun.

People born on 29 February have a birthday once every four years!

Leap Years

A calendar year is 365 days in length, but the solar year is slightly longer. So, every four years, an extra day is added to the calendar year in February, the shortest month. These 366-day years are called leap years.

Earth's Tilt

As the Earth moves around the Sun, parts of the Earth receive different amounts of sunlight at different times of the year. This is because the Earth's axis is tilted **at an angle**. This tilt is the reason the Earth has seasons.

The Earth's axis stays tilted at an angle of 23.45 degrees.

We can spend longer outside in summer because we have more hours of daylight.

Four Different Seasons

In most places around the world the year is divided into four seasons: spring, summer, autumn and winter. Each season has different weather, temperatures and hours of daylight. For example, summer has sunny weather with high temperatures and many hours of daylight. Winter is often cloudy with cool temperatures and fewer daylight hours.

How Seasons are Created

Different seasons occur because of the tilt of the Earth's axis. The tilt of the Earth's axis never changes. As the Earth moves around the Sun during the year, either the top half or the bottom half of the Earth is tilted towards the Sun. The top half of the Earth is called the Northern **Hemisphere** and the bottom half is called the Southern Hemisphere. When a hemisphere is tilted towards the Sun, it is summer there. When a hemisphere is tilted away from the Sun, it is winter there.

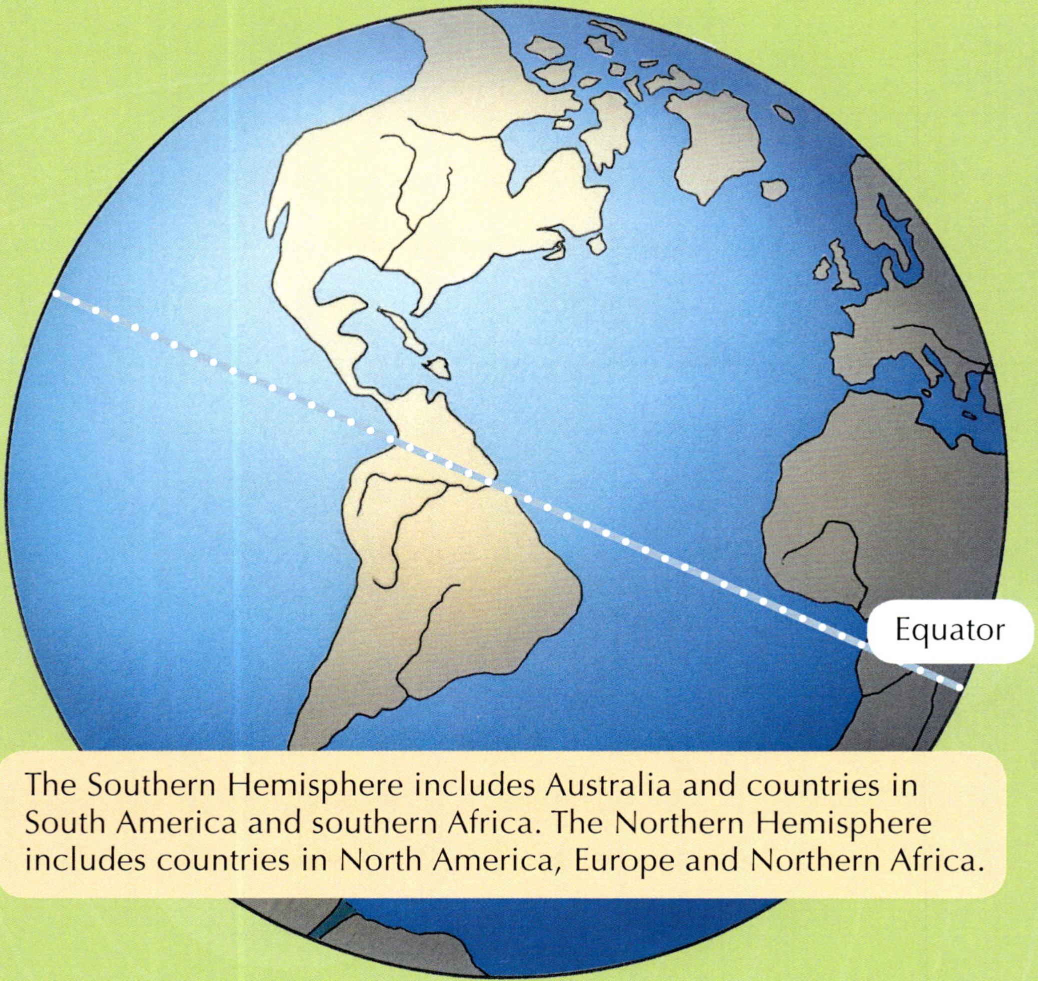

The Southern Hemisphere includes Australia and countries in South America and southern Africa. The Northern Hemisphere includes countries in North America, Europe and Northern Africa.

In summer a hemisphere is angled towards the Sun. The daylight hours are longer, and the air temperatures are hotter because the sunlight hits it directly.

In winter a hemisphere is tilted away from the Sun, so there are fewer hours of daylight. The days are shorter and colder, because the sunlight hits that part of the Earth at an angle, so it is less strong.

Here, the Northern Hemisphere is experiencing summer because it is tilted towards the Sun. The Southern Hemisphere is experiencing winter.

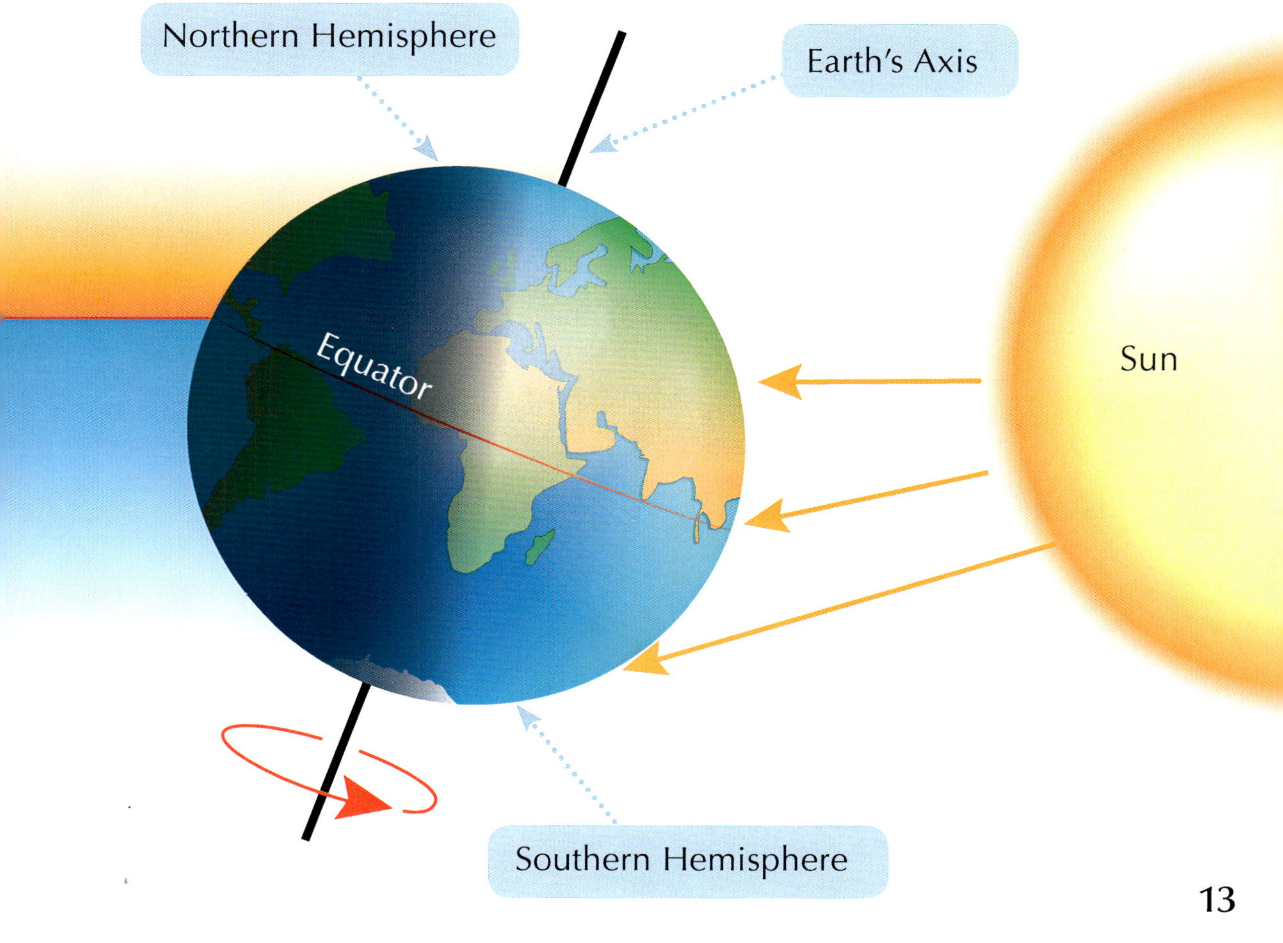

Seasons in the Polar Regions

The North and South Poles experience extreme seasons of winter and summer because of the Earth's tilt. When the North Pole is tilted away from the Sun, the area does not receive any direct sunlight from October to March. It is dark all day for nearly three months. At the same time of year, the South Pole is tilted towards the sun. It is light all day and night for nearly three months.

Tromso during the day in summer

People who live in the town of Tromso, Norway, have very dark winters and they may not see the sun for 60 days!

Tromso during the day in winter

On the equator, the day is approximately the same length all year round – about 12 hours.

Seasons near the Equator

The equator is an imaginary line that separates the Northern Hemisphere from the Southern Hemisphere at the Earth's widest point. Places that are close to the equator get nearly the same amount of sunlight all year. In some places on the equator, there is a very warm rainy season and a cooler, drier time of the year.

Measuring Time

Ancient cultures developed ways of measuring and describing time. They named the seasons and tracked time using calendars. This helped them predict what would happen and when.

Knowing the seasons

It was very important to know what season it was and when seasons would change. Finding and growing different foods depended very much on the seasons. Farming societies needed to plant crops in spring, and harvest them in the autumn. Societies based on hunting and gathering needed to know when to move from one place to another for food.

The Inca people used the sun to work out when to plant and harvest corn.

The ancient Mayan calendar is divided into 19 months.

Inventing Calendars

As the Earth moves around the Sun, the stars in the night sky also appear to move. Some ancient societies created calendars by tracking this movement of the stars in the night sky. One such society was the Mayans from central America. Some ancient societies also used the Moon to track time and create calendars.

Some ancient calendars are still used to work out the date of traditional or religious celebrations. For example, the Chinese traditional calendar is used to work out the start and end dates of Chinese New Year.

The Chinese traditional calendar relates to the position of the Moon. It is still used to work out when Chinese New Year is celebrated.

The calendar developed by Julius Caesar was called the Julian calendar.

Calendars are useful for keeping track of appointments, events and birthdays!

The Modern Calendar

The calendar that most countries have today was first used in 1582. It is based on a calendar developed by the Roman Emperor, Julius Caesar, in the year 46 BCE.

Understanding Earth's Movement

Since the earliest times, people have tried to understand the world around them. Measuring and describing night and day, the seasons and the calendar year has always been hugely important to humans. For most of history, though, humans believed that the Sun circled the Earth, instead of the other way around. They were unable to connect day, night, seasons and years with the Earth's movement. But in the 1500s and 1600s, the calculations of Nicolaus Copernicus and the telescope developed by Galileo Galilei allowed scientists to prove that the Earth moves around the Sun.

Copernicus (left) was a Polish astronomer and Galileo (right) was an Italian scientist and mathematician.

Earth's Sun is just one star among billions in the universe.

We now understand that the Earth moves around the sun. It spins on its axis and gives us day and night. The Earth's tilt creates the seasons in many parts of the world.

Glossary

at an angle slanting away from a straight line

axis an imaginary line around which something, such as the Earth, spins

calendar a system of measuring time, especially over months and years

hemisphere half of a sphere (a ball-shaped object)

orbits circles or moves around something

rotation one complete turn around an axis

solar relating to or describing the Sun

Index

After Reading

Let's Think About It

- What is the most fascinating fact you read in this book?
- Which diagram did you find the most interesting? Why?
- Why is it important to learn about Earth?

Let's Talk About It

Turn to your partner and discuss.

- The most fascinating fact I read was ...
- The most interesting diagram ...
- I think it is important to learn about Earth because ...

How are your answers the same or different?